Big Hole River

BIG HOLE RIVER

Steve Probasco

Frank Amato

PORTLAND

River Journal

Volume 3, Number 3, 1995

ABOUT THE AUTHOR

Steve Probasco is a full time writer/photographer living in Raymond, Washington. Steve's articles and photography appear regularly in several U.S., Canadian and British publications, and he is the Washington Editor for "The Outdoor Journal," a syndicated radio program. Steve is the author of a previous River Journal; Yakima River, Volume 2, Number 2. In addition, Steve is the author of one book and one video on fly tying, with several other works in progress. He is a seminar speaker/fly tier for Ed Rice's International Sportsmen's Expositions, as well as a seminar speaker/fly tier at the Federation of Fly Fishers International Fly Fishing Show.

◆

Acknowledgments

Many thanks to Dick Vincent, Regional Fisheries Manager for the Montana Department of Fish, Wildlife and Parks, for providing much of the statistical information in this River Journal. Dick Oswald, Big Hole Biologist for the Department, for providing data on fish populations, habitat information, etc. Thanks also to my fishing partners who so diligently "hung out" while I photographed everything in sight. All flies in the plate, with the exception of Steve's Salmon Fly and the Bow River Bugger, were provided by Spirit River, Inc. in Roseburg, Oregon (503)440-6916.

◆

Editors: Frank Amato—Kim Koch

Subscriptions:
Softbound: $29.90 for one year (four issues)
$55.00 for two years
Hardbound Limited Editions: $80.00 one year, $150.00 for two years

Design: Joyce Herbst
Photography: Steve Probasco unless otherwise noted
Map: Tony Amato   Flyplates: Jim Schollmeyer
Printed in Hong Kong
Softbound ISBN:1-57188-006-2, Hardbound ISBN:1-57188-007-0
(Hardbound Edition Limited to 500 Copies)

BIG HOLE RIVER

(Wisdom to Twin Bridges)

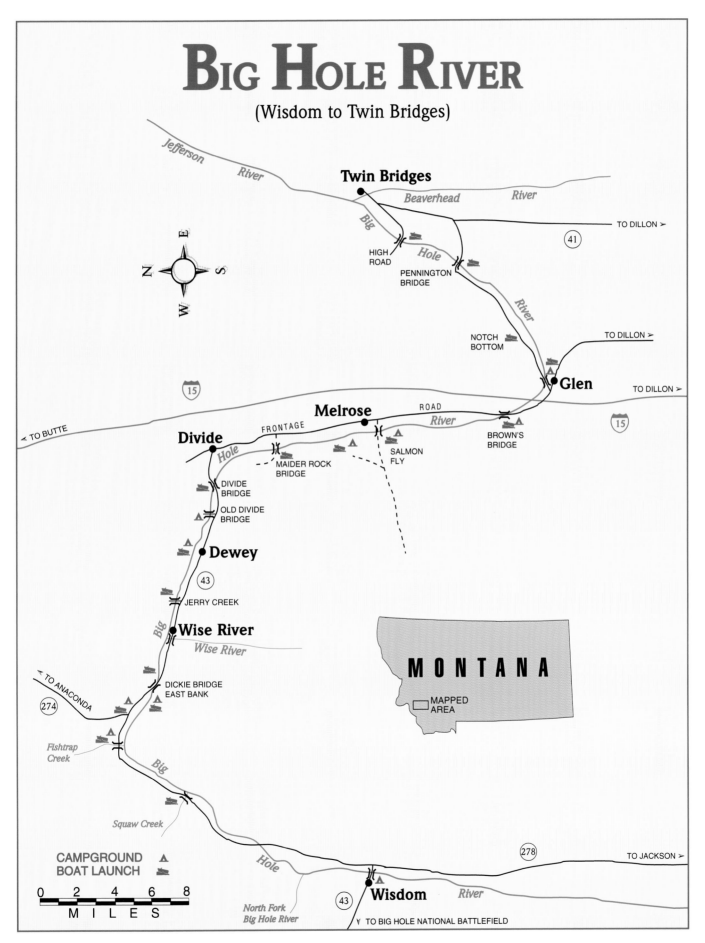

Jefferson River

Twin Bridges

Beaverhead River

TO DILLON
(41)

Big

HIGH ROAD

Hole

PENNINGTON BRIDGE

NOTCH BOTTOM

River

TO DILLON

Glen

TO DILLON

(15)

N E S W

(15)

Melrose

ROAD

Divide

FRONTAGE

River

BROWN'S BRIDGE

TO BUTTE

Hole

MAIDER ROCK BRIDGE

SALMON FLY

DIVIDE BRIDGE

OLD DIVIDE BRIDGE

Dewey

(43)

JERRY CREEK

Big

Wise River

Wise River

TO ANACONDA

DICKIE BRIDGE EAST BANK

(274)

MONTANA

Fishtrap Creek

Big

MAPPED AREA

Squaw Creek

CAMPGROUND
BOAT LAUNCH

Big

(278)

TO JACKSON

0 2 4 6 8
M I L E S

Hole

(43) Wisdom

River

North Fork
Big Hole River

TO BIG HOLE NATIONAL BATTLEFIELD

The Big Hole River near its source in the Beaverhead Mountains.

BIG HOLE RIVER

---

*O*FF TO THE RIGHT, MT. HAGGIN, MT. EVANS AND the other 10,000-foot peaks of the Anaconda Range stand towering above French Creek, a tributary of the Big Hole, as it winds in a southerly direction through high rangeland en route to the Big Hole Valley below. Highway 274 abruptly levels at its junction with State Highway 43, which parallels the Big Hole River through this part of the valley. The Big Hole River can be reached via this route from Anaconda to the north, east or west via Highway 43, and from Interstate 15, the north/south route.

The Big Hole River comes to life in the Beaverhead Mountains south of Jackson, Montana, as the outlet of Skinner Lake, elevation 7,340 feet. Throughout the 155.6 miles it flows, the Big Hole takes on many faces. From its beginning as a small mountain stream, the Big Hole flows north to Wisdom, where it gains strength by joining with the North Fork and flows north-easterly for about 25 miles. It then flows 27 miles eastward past Wise River and Divide, gaining more volume from several creeks, as well as Wise River itself. At Divide the river changes course to the south and is paralleled by Interstate 15 for 17 miles. Then, at Glen the Big Hole heads southeast for its remaining 25 miles to the point where it joins the Beaverhead, and forms the Jefferson River, near Twin Bridges, Montana, at an elevation of 4,600 feet.

Much of the Big Hole's water comes from the Beaverhead, Pioneer and Anaconda Mountains. With the drought this part of Montana (as well as much of the western U.S.) has been experiencing over the last several years, water flows on this river have been depressed, and is especially noticeable during the late summer and fall months. In fact, during the summer of 1994, the Big Hole was closed to fishing for a few months due to low flows and high water temperatures. It is unknown, as of this writing, what effect the situation had on the Big Hole's trout.

According to Dick Oswald, Fisheries Biologist for the Department of Fish, Wildlife and Parks, there was probably a fish kill resulting from the low flows of '94, but the extent won't be known until spring when electrofishing is done. This was not the first time the river has been closed for this reason and it probably won't be the last. But the Big Hole's trout have been resilient in the past. A normal snowpack and spring runoff would certainly be welcome here.

Fishing on the Big Hole River has always been popular. This river is one of Montana's best, with a diversity that's hard to match. The Big Hole hosts rainbow, brown, cutthroat and brook trout. Rocky Mountain whitefish are also present, as well as the last fluvial (river-dwelling) population of grayling in the United States, outside of Alaska, of course.

Much of the land bordering the Big Hole River is privately owned, so floating the river will let you cover the greatest amount of water. There are several stretches with good bank access for fishermen, and I will talk about those areas in detail later in this journal. But by boat or from the bank, the Big Hole offers anglers willing to put in the time, a real treat.

The Big Hole is fishable from its source down to its confluence with the Beaverhead. This river takes on many faces throughout its journey; from mountain stream, to meadow stream, tumbling through a canyon and then on to a broad slow-moving river meandering through farmland. The Big Hole has a variety of water that can be fished using a variety of methods. The Montana Department of Fish, Wildlife and Parks manages

The north fork of the Big Hole and the site of the Nez Percé Battle of the Big Hole, 1877.

the Big Hole fisheries in several segments, with slot limits, gear restrictions, and regulations suited, they believe, to best manage the fish in each segment. More on this later.

Overall, the Big Hole River is a gem—one of the west's best, and highly praised for its trout fisheries. But faced with the drought of the past several years, irresponsible water usage and grazing practices by some ranchers, and somewhat liberal angling regulations in comparison to many blue ribbon fisheries, I believe the Big Hole needs some special and thoughtful consideration if it is to continue at its present status, as one of Montana's best trout streams.

Battle of the Big Hole

IN THE MID-1800S, GOLD MINERS AND SETTLERS began moving west and onto the homelands of the Nez Percé Indians. The Nez Percé were peaceful people and in 1855, to avoid conflict, signed a treaty that confined them to a large reservation located on their ancestral land, that area is where Washington, Oregon and Idaho meet.

In 1860 gold was discovered on the reservation and in 1863 settlers and miners forced a new treaty reducing the reservation down to one-tenth its original size. Only those chiefs whose land lay within the smaller reservation signed this treaty. The five bands of Indians whose land fell outside the new boundary

refused. These five bands became known as the "non-treaty" Nez Percé.

The non-treaty Indians remained on their land until 1877, when General Oliver O. Howard was instructed to enforce the new treaty. Reluctantly the chiefs agreed to the treaty and made way towards the reservation. On June 15, a few young warriors attacked several settlers who had earlier cheated or killed members of their families. Other warriors eventually joined in and ended up killing 17 settlers in two days. Most of the non-treaty Nez Percé fled, fearing retaliation.

The non-treaty Indians were now on the run, trying desperately to avoid the army. It all came to a head on July 11 when the Indians and the army fought for two days near Idaho's Clearwater River. The Nez Percé fled, and under the leadership of Chief Looking Glass, began a 1,300 mile journey over the Bitterroot Mountains and through the Montana Territory. General Howard was in close pursuit.

On the morning of August 7, 1877, the Nez Percé set up camp along the banks of the North Fork of the Big Hole River. Chief Looking Glass felt they were far enough ahead of General Howard that they would be safe, and didn't post guards around the camp. Little did Looking Glass know but Colonel John Gibbon and 162 men of the 7th U.S. Infantry out of Fort Shaw and four other western Montana forts, along with several volunteers, had joined the pursuit.

Gibbon's scouts spotted the tepees along the river on August 8th. The next morning the soldiers were preparing to attack at first light when an Indian who was out checking horses stumbled into the soldiers' position and was shot, starting the battle before dawn. The soldiers crossed the river and indiscriminately began shooting men, women and children.

Eventually, Nez Percé snipers pushed the soldiers back across the river and into a stand of pine trees where they remained for the next 24 hours. In the early hours of August 10th, the Nez Percé warriors fired a barrage of shots and joined the rest of their band who had already broke camp and were headed south.

The Battle of the Big Hole, as this episode was to become known, was the bloodiest battle of the Nez Percé War of 1877. Sixty to ninety Nez Percé were killed, at least half of which were women, children and old people. The infantry losses totaled 29 dead and 40 wounded.

After the Battle of the Big Hole the Nez Percé eventually made way towards Canada where they hoped to join forces with Sitting Bull. On September 30, only 40-miles south of the Canadian border, the Nez Percé came under attack by army troops under the command of Nelson A. Miles. After five days of fighting, and the deaths of four chiefs (including Looking Glass), the battle was over. Chief Joseph surrendered to Miles. Upon surrendering, Chief Joseph reportedly spoke to Colonel Miles the famous words: "Hear me, my chiefs, I am, tired; my heart is sick and sad. From where the sun now stands I will fight no more forever."

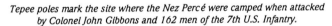

A lone antelope near the frontage road close to Divide.

Tepee poles mark the site where the Nez Percé were camped when attacked by Colonel John Gibbons and 162 men of the 7th U.S. Infantry.

Big Hole History

SETTLERS STARTED ARRIVING IN THE BIG HOLE VALLEY immediately after the Nez Percé battle. But before the settlers came, the Lewis and Clark Expedition passed through the valley in early August, 1805. Having already named the Jefferson River after their President and expedition sponsor, the party reached what Captain Lewis described as the forks of the Jefferson. The explorers named the forks for President Jefferson's three cardinal virtues—Philosophy, Philanthropy, and Wisdom. The first river eventually went back to its Indian name, Beaverhead. Philanthropy eventually became known as the Stinking Water, and is now the Ruby River. The northerly fork Lewis personally named Wisdom River is now known as the Big Hole.

In the *Journals of Lewis and Clark*, they make mention of the low water level of the Big Hole, and the difficulty of navigation by boat. On Saturday, August 3rd, 1805, a passage read, "The men were so much fortiegued today that they wished much that navigation was at an end that they might go by land."

The Shoshone Indians knew the Big Hole Valley as Ground Squirrel Valley, and the Land of the Big Snows. Lewis and Clark called it Hot Springs Valley. Later it was to become known as the Valley of 10,000 Haystacks. It was the trappers who probably came up with the name "Big Hole" by describing the valley it drains.

Following page: The Big Hole River in the fall is the most colorful of Montana's blue ribbon rivers. Paul Updike photo.

An average Montana grayling from the upper river near the town of Wisdom.

Even before the battle with the Nez Percé, white men were starting to make their presence known along the Big Hole. In 1865, the Lott brothers built toll bridges across the Beaverhead and Big Hole Rivers, and Twin Bridges was born. In 1873, further upstream a post office was built along the river and given the name Divide. Less than ten years later, Divide was to become a way-station and livestock shipping point to Butte, via the Union Pacific Railroad.

Just after the battle several small communities sprouted along the Big Hole River. First came Dewey, which was named for D.S. Dewey, an early rancher. Dewey first began as a lumber camp and later became a mining town when gold was discovered in Quartz Hill Gulch in 1877. In 1878, the Willis Stage Station and post office appeared. When the Union Pacific Railroad arrived the name was changed to Glen. And in 1882, a young couple moved into a cabin at "The Crossing," which was the point where stage routes met; south to Idaho, west over the Bitterroot Mountains and north to Butte. Two years later there were enough residents to build a post office and the town became known as Wisdom.

More communities eventually followed, and when the gold ran out the Big Hole Valley was well established as a producer of top-quality hay. In 1909 two local farmers invented a hay stacker known as the Sunny Slope Slide ("Beaver-slide") Hay Stacker. Several of these intriguing structures can be seen today in the hay fields up the Big Hole Valley.

Ranching and hay farming are big-business in the Big Hole Valley today. The river provides irrigation for the fertile land, and it has since the settlers arrived. But during the past several drought years irresponsible and careless use of the Big Hole's

water by some, has, in part, contributed to the drought-related damage to the stream and its fish. More on this later.

Angling has always been a draw to the Big Hole. Dewey Flats was once a destination for fishermen from Butte, which was a long day's ride by horseback. Today the Big Hole hosts visitors from all over the country. The "Hole," as it is known by those who frequent it, is a blue ribbon fishery, one of Montana's finest.

Grayling in the Big Hole

*F*ROM OUR STANCE ON THE HIGH BANK OVERLOOKing the river, fish could be seen rising below a riffle that emptied into a small pool. We couldn't tell what they were, but they seemed to be in a frenzy, feeding on something, probably the small caddis that were flying all around. As we slid and stumbled down the bank I was hoping the fish to be rainbows sucking up the caddisflies. It was a pleasant surprise when my first cast revealed the risers to be grayling, the largest of which ran about 12 inches.

The native stream-dwelling grayling of the Big Hole are the last in the lower 48 states. These grayling are clinging to a difficult existence, battling habitat destruction, natural drought, agricultural dewatering, pollution, and competition with other fish.

Brook trout, which are actually char, were introduced into the upper Big Hole in the 1930s. The introduction of these brookies probably had the greatest detrimental effect on the grayling population. Lower on the river, the introduction of rainbows and brown trout took their toll also. Recent studies suggest that grayling don't compete well with other fish. To help in the competition issue between the brookies and grayling, the Department of Fish, Wildlife and Parks encourages a high harvest rate of the brookies with a 20 fish or 10 pound limit.

Grayling used to be widely distributed in the upper Missouri River system, but today, the upper Big Hole hosts the last of these fish. Will man let them survive, or will we interfere with the ecosystem to the point where they disappear forever?

Research has found that the Big Hole grayling are genetically different than other grayling. And since these grayling are the last of their kind, management emphasis is a special concern. The grayling are listed as a "Species of Special Concern" by the Montana Department of Fish, Wildlife and Parks and the potential exists for the species to be classified as threatened or endangered under federal law.

Recent population surveys of the grayling on the upper Big Hole are low, with estimates ranging from 35 to 60 fish per mile. It wasn't until 1988 that fishing regulations for the grayling were changed to catch-and-release of all grayling. Over the past few years, the grayling population has been relatively stable, even under the drought conditions.

Mature Big Hole grayling usually run between 8 and 12 inches, with a few larger fish. At present, there is a plan to reintroduce grayling back into other Missouri River tributaries. As of this writing they have been reintroduced into the Gallatin River,

with several more target rivers slated for plantings in the future. It will be interesting to follow this project as it develops.

Grayling densities on the Big Hole are highest near the town of Wisdom, and thin out the further downstream you go. Seldom are grayling caught below Divide.

The Montana Department of Fish, Wildlife and Parks is very dedicated to the survival of the Big Hole grayling. The Department's highest priority is protecting and enhancing grayling populations. Management practices are under constant evaluation, and the Department is working closely with the U.S Geological Survey (USGS), the Bureau of Land Management (BLM), ranchers and other land users to ensure water quality and develop plans for the preservation of these fish; the last of their kind.

The Big Hole By Sections

*I*T WAS A CLOUDY MAY MORNING, WITH PERIODS OF intense, yet brief rain showers. The temperature hovered in the mid-thirties. The snow level was way down and with each clearing of the clouds, the surrounding mountains could clearly be seen—plastered white with snow. Just as winter arrives early in the Big Hole Valley, spring is sometimes slow in arriving also.

The long drive from Washington state made my fishing part-

Farmland and the Beaverhead Mountains near Jackson, on the upper Big Hole.

Yellow willows line the riffles of the Madin Rock section of the Big Hole River. Paul Updike photo.

Wildflowers along the upper river in May.

◆

along the Big Hole through this part of the valley. When the water is up, the section of river here is ribboned, with several, fairly slow-moving channels. Nothing was hatching—the weather was too severe. So we tied small nymphs to our tippets and began bouncing the bottom of the deeper runs.

Bracing ourselves against the wind, casts were tough, but we caught the occasional trout. To our nymphs fell a mixture of small rainbows, brookies and also grayling. This was my first time catching grayling outside of Alaska, the Yukon or the Northwest Territories and, even though these Big Hole grayling were much smaller than those encountered up north, catching them meant so much more, knowing that these grayling are the last of their kind. Very carefully we slipped each grayling back into the river.

Covering about one-half-mile of stream, we worked over every likely piece of water with our nymphs. Before leaving this stretch I also caught a small cutthroat. The weather was atrocious, yet the fish came freely. Eventually we were persuaded by the storm to move further downstream. Finding a somewhat sheltered area we again began casting a variety of small nymphs into fishy looking water. Before calling it quits in this spot we hooked mountain whitefish, rainbow and brown trout. In just a few short hours, our flies took every species of game fish the Big Hole had to offer. I was impressed.

One can just as easily fish a whole day on the Big Hole and get skunked! The trout can be as difficult and as frustrating as on any spring creek or they can be incredibly easy. One thing is certain, the Big Hole and its fishing is changing. In general, the fish are getting a lot smarter. The angler must pay close attention to hatches and presentation in order to be successful.

ners and me determined to fish the river, even if we froze our fannies off in the process, which, the way the weather was looking seemed a not too unrealistic possibility. We donned all of our cold weather gear, heavy neoprene waders, and slipped into the icy waters of the middle Big Hole River.

We were fishing a section of river not too far from the point where the road from Anaconda joins Highway 43, which runs

◆

An average brook trout taken in the upper river near Wisdom. Brook trout are plentiful in the upper river and its tributaries.

15

In 1989 the Montana Department of Fish, Wildlife and Parks, developed a Fisheries Management Plan for Region 3. This five year Fisheries Management Plan takes a close look at every aspect of the Big Hole fishery. The Department is working very hard to maintain the blue ribbon status of this stream, fighting what seems at times, a losing battle. Of utmost concern is protecting the fragile grayling population.

According to the study conducted by the Department, numbers of large fish, those 20-inch-plus rainbows and browns, are on the decline. This decline is most likely due to angler harvest of the large fish, sedimentation of spawning habitat, erosion of streambanks and summer dewatering. It is my opinion that all of the problems mentioned can be corrected, if the desire and fortitude of all land and water users is there and together they work towards that goal, and if appropriate decisions are made by those who can make them.

In this study the Department has broken the Big Hole down into four management reaches. Each reach is managed in a different manner, working closely with the U.S. Forest Service, the Bureau of Land Management, and private land/water users in an effort to best manage the fishery as a whole.

I have broken the river down into sections myself, as I talk of the fishing found in the different reaches. I will mention the Department's management plan for each section, starting at the river's source.

Source to Wisdom

Out of sheer curiosity I drove to Jackson and followed the Big Hole into the mountains. At this point the river was nothing more than a small stream. The road had long since turned to gravel, and wound deep into the Beaverhead Mountains. At a couple of points the road crossed the stream. Not on this pioneering venture, but on a later trip I fished the river in these places. I found only small brookies and because of the harsh environment, that's likely all you will find here. Continuing on my journey I followed the stream, smashing through snow drifts all the way to its source, Skinner Lake.

Backtracking downstream, I did a little fishing once I got out of the mountains. It wasn't until I got closer to the town of Jackson that I encountered my first grayling. Casting dry flies to all of the suspecting water eventually produced one of these magnificent fish, with their sail-like dorsal fin, covered with brilliant turquoise spots. When a grayling is hooked, its silvery body seems to intensify and shimmer as you bring it in close. Even if it were legal to keep grayling here, it would be a crime against nature, as there are very few of them left.

Continuing to fish the upper river I encountered stretches where I couldn't keep the brookies off. They seemed to be everywhere. At first, subconsciously I released them all back into the stream, probably because I usually release all of the fish I catch.

Ken Bamford fishes a section of the middle Big Hole River during the spring, with a view up the Big Hole Valley.

An afternoon thunderstorm rattles through the mountains to the north of the Big Hole Valley.

And then I remembered the concern that the brookies are competing with the dwindling grayling population and that the Department encourages the harvest of them. I left the stream that day with a bag full of tasty little brook trout and a clean conscience.

The upper river from Jackson to Wisdom is fishable for smaller fish, mostly grayling, brook, and cutthroat trout. This is not a heavily-fished stretch of river as it runs through private land, has heavy streamside vegetation (willows) and is difficult to float. For the most part the fish found here are not bothered, save for the occasional moose stomping up the stream.

The closer you get to Wisdom, the more grayling you will find. It is near Wisdom where the largest concentrations of these fish are found and, if you can gain access to the water, these gluttonous feeders will take nearly any dry fly or nymph you throw at them.

Wisdom to Pintler Creek

Around Wisdom the Big Hole becomes a meandering meadow-type stream. At high water, floating the upper section can be dangerous due to sharp bends and barbed-wire fences that cross the river. During periods of low flow this section is difficult to float, simply due to the lack of water. You end up doing a lot of boat pushing and pulling.

In this section of the river you will find brook and cutthroat trout as well as a few rainbows. The grayling, which are most

numerous near Wisdom start to thin the further downstream you go. All species found in this part of the river are on the small size, in comparison with the river downstream.

Fishing regulations sign along the banks of the Big Hole.

- **ATTENTION ANGLERS** -
BIG HOLE RIVER
SPECIAL REGULATIONS

GRAYLING - Catch and release in river and all tributary streams
DICKIE BRIDGE TO MELROSE BRIDGE - 3 trout per day under 13 inches and one trout over 22 inches (3rd Saturday in May through November), Artificial lures only.
EXTENDED WHITEFISH AND CATCH - AND - RELEASE TROUT SEASON - December 1 to 3rd Saturday in May with maggots and/or artificial lures **except** Divide dam to Melrose bridge which is closed to **all** fishing from December 1 to 3rd Saturday in May
CHECK YOUR REGULATIONS PAMPHLET

Montana Department of Fish, Wildlife & Parks

17

Pintler Creek to Dickey Bridge

This section of the Big Hole is slow moving and is paralleled by Highway 43 making for great access. Much of this access is via BLM land, where public lands meet the river. Fish concentrations will be whitefish, brook, rainbow and cutthroat trout, with thinning grayling populations. A few brown trout start to appear from Fishtrap on downstream, but will generally be on the small size.

A few miles downstream from Fishtrap you come to Sportsman Park. For several years this area was planted annually with 3,000 catchable-size rainbow trout, by request of the Anaconda Sportman Club which owns the facility. This stocking was discontinued in 1989 when it was determined by the Department of Fish, Wildlife and Parks that the hatchery fish actually depress wild fish populations, and that the stocked rainbows here were probably having a negative impact on the grayling.

Floating this section of the river is straightforward, with few obstacles. This is a popular section in the early season when there is plenty of water for navigation.

The fish found in this section of river start to increase in size, and although the blue ribbon section of the Big Hole is further downstream, you can sometimes be surprised with a big fish. At times of a good hatch, the slow water found in this part of the river can be a real pleasure to fish.

Dickey Bridge to Divide

The game trail leading down to the river was steep. Below, in the fading evening light, riseforms could be seen covering the flat, tailout of the pool. I carefully waded into the river and began casting a small adult midge pattern to the rising fish.

There are those times with fly fishing when everything seems to go "just right" and, this was one of those times. Nearly every drag-free float of my fly produced either a rainbow, small grayling or mountain whitefish. It was in total darkness that I made my way back up the game trail. Even after reaching my car, I could still hear the occasional splash of rising fish.

The section of the river between Dickey Bridge and Divide includes a stretch where the 'Hole runs through a scenic canyon, with boulders, pools, riffles and faster current than any other section of the river. This is my favorite part of the Big Hole. Bank access is good, with several parking areas along the canyon and trails leading down to the river. Moderate whitewater skills are needed if you plan on floating this stretch of class II-III (depending on flow) water.

Rainbows are the dominant species here, but browns and whitefish are also numerous, with a few brookies and grayling taken at times. Special regulations are in effect for this part of the river. These regulations include the harvest of four fish, three under 13 inches and one over 22 inches. All grayling must be released here, just as in all parts of the Big Hole and its tributaries.

Although rainbows are the most prevalent in this section,

Jordan Probasco with a respectable rainbow taken in the Big Hole River below the town of Melrose.

This section of the Big Hole, like further upstream, flows mostly through private farm and rangeland. During the fall when water flows are typically down, the river here can become very slow and stagnant. Cattle grazing along the banks of the river here are a cause for concern.

Heavy livestock concentrations along a river inevitably results in vegetation removal and destruction of the stream banks. Cattle tramping around in a river causes further damage and ultimately eliminates holding water for the fish. Bacteria levels increase with livestock waste entering the river. And since we know grayling need pure, clean water for survival, this is obviously not good.

It seems to this writer that with the careless livestock grazing practices that still take place on the Big Hole, along with the severe dewatering during the fall, disaster for grayling can- not be too far off. I hope I am wrong!

Previous page: Huge brown trout on their spawning migration can sometimes be seen going upstream in the low water of fall here at Melrose.
Paul Updike photo.

and average under 13 inches in length, a recent study by the Department revealed a fair number of rainbows in the 16 to 20 inch range, with a few trophy-sized rainbow in the five to seven pound range.

Brown trout here, although they make up a small percentage (7-13%) of the trout population, are often large. Dick Oswald, Fisheries Biologist for the Department told me that electrofishing indicates a good population of brown trout in the 5 to 10 pound range, with a few specimens into the mid-teens.

For floaters, there are river access points at Dickey Bridge, Jerry Creek, Dewey, the Old Divide Bridge and at the Divide Bridge. If floating all the way to the Divide Bridge there is a special hazard to be aware of at the Big Hole Pumping Station. Since 1900, this pumping station has been supplying about half of Butte's water supply during the summer. It has been reported that up to 14 million gallons, or 20 cfs of river per day flow through wooden pipelines 20 air-miles to the north over the Continental Divide. The hazard here is the diversion weir. It has a very treacherous backwash which has claimed several lives. Pay strict attention to the signs posted on the bridge upstream. You must portage (left).

Divide to Glen

It was mid-summer and fishing was slow. No, it was slower than slow. It was dead. The only action for the past several days had been during a narrow window of time just before dark. If you had a streamer in the water during this time, you caught fish. Brown trout to 20 inches made a long, fishless day a little more acceptable.

One evening my two boys, my father-in-law and I walked from our camp up to the bend upstream from Brown's Bridge, below Melrose. Spreading out, we methodically cast streamers into the deeper water against the far side of the stream and stripped our fast-sinking tips back at a rapid pace to avoid snagging the moss-covered rocks. Several of my flies fell to the rocks, but at least I was getting my fly down into fish territory. Anyway, at one point I snagged solidly and helplessly into the rocks—or so I thought. After a couple of sharp tugs of the rod, my rock took off.

Living on the Pacific Coast, I do plenty of steelhead fishing. Had I not known better I would have sworn that I had a steelhead on my line. The powerful runs and obstinate head shaking

Jack Elefritz fishing a drift on a float from Salmon Fly to Brown's Bridge.

The lower Big Hole upstream from the High Road Bridge during the fall of 1994.

was very much like that of fresh-from-the-ocean steelhead. After only a few short blasts, the fish spit my fly. Shaken, I headed back to camp, knowing good and well that I probably lost a trophy brown trout, quite possibly the largest I have ever hooked in a river.

The section of the Big Hole from Divide to Glen is considered the blue ribbon stretch and is the most heavily fished section of the river. There is little bank access here, so floating is pretty much the rule. Floaters can launch at the Divide Bridge or at either of the two Maiden Rock accesses. The upper Maiden Rock access is provided by the Bureau of Land Management, and the lower by the Department of Fish, Wildlife and Parks. The canyon through which the river flows near Maiden Rock can be bouncy during high water and floaters should have the skills to negotiate short stretches of Class II-III water.

Rainbows predominate the reaches near Divide, while browns predominate once you get closer to Melrose. In this section it is possible to hook a trophy of either species. Estimates vary, and change due to drought mortality, but recently, there was reported to be in the neighborhood of 3,000 fish per mile in this section of the Big Hole River.

In 1981 the segment of river between Divide and Melrose was placed under a special "slot limit" regulations that requires all trout between 13 and 22 inches be released. The daily bag limit is three fish under 13 inches and one over 22 inches. This special regulation section is open to fishing during Montana's standard fishing season only, from the third Saturday in May through November 30th. Fishing gear is restricted to the use of artificial flies and lures.

At present, from Melrose down to Glen, and beyond, the 'Hole falls under the standard Montana river regulations with a limit of five fish, only one of which can be over 18 inches, with no gear restrictions. This section also has an extended whitefish season which is open from December 1st to the 3rd Saturday in May. All trout caught must be released. The Department is keeping a close watch on this section of the Big Hole, and strong public support as well as Department data collected, could extend the "slot limit" regulation further downstream from Melrose in the near future.

The river from Melrose to Brown's Bridge is a pleasant, slow-paced stretch which flows through farmland, without much bank access. One can walk downstream a ways from the Salmon

Fly Campground near Melrose, or upstream from the campground at Brown's Bridge, but both offer very limited access. Floating is the best way to go, and will take you through some relatively isolated water, scattered with many beautiful stretches of river, including several "big brown" hideouts.

Glen to High Road

It is a short float from Brown's Bridge to Glen. The float from Glen to High Road, near the confluence of the Big Hole and Beaverhead Rivers is probably the least floated section of the 'Hole. Access is poor, the river is braided with numerous sweeps, and during low water periods, many channels may be impassable, and sometimes you can't buy a fish, save for the occasional whitefish.

There are brown trout here, and some are very large. It is during spring and early summer when your chances are best at making contact with them. When the water is low, this section of river is best enjoyed for the float, that is if there is enough water to do so. When there is, it is a pleasant, gentle drift through the cottonwood bottom lands.

One final note on fishing the Big Hole. There are voluntary census stations located at key access sites along the river. Anglers are asked to fill out cards with information about how many grayling they hook and release. And keep in mind, all grayling caught on the Big Hole and its tributaries must be released unharmed.

Fishing Through the Seasons

*T*HE BIG HOLE IS A RIVER IN WHICH FISHING IS VERY much influenced by the seasons. Fluctuation in water flow, and consequently high water temperatures, is the key reason the fishing drops off and this can be attributed to a variety of reasons. The biggest reason for lack of flow on the Big Hole is the drought that southwest Montana, as well as the rest of the western United States, has been experiencing for the past several years.

Water flow information is available at any given time from the USGS in Helena (406) 449-5263. The gauging station is located between Melrose and Glen, and when planning a float trip down the Big Hole it is a good idea to call first. A record of flow on the Big Hole has been in effect since 1923. The maximum flow ever measured on the river was 23,000 cfs in 1927, but this was related to a dam failure. The next highest flow on record was recorded in June of 1972, at 14,300 cfs. The lowest flow ever recorded was 49 cfs in August of 1931. Records show that the average flow of the Big Hole over a 64 year period was 1,162 cfs.

To put the minimum flow figure in perspective, when the Big Hole was closed to fishing for a few months starting in August of 1994, the flow was measured at the Melrose gauge around 130 cfs according to the USGS. However, according to Dick Oswald of the Department, a couple of times during the fall of

A nice rainbow comes to net in the Big Hole River in the Melrose area.

A hefty rainbow trout feeding in the middle Big Hole.

◆

'94 there were stretches on the upper river when flows were nearly as low as the all-time low recorded in 1931.

At the time of this writing, seasons and fishing regulations on the Big Hole are as follows. Tributaries only, upstream from the Divide Dam are open for brook trout the entire year. An extended whitefish season and catch-and-release for trout is in effect December 1 to the third Saturday in May, except from the Divide Dam to the Melrose Bridge where the fishing is closed during this time. From Dickey Bridge to the Melrose Bridge there is a "slot limit" in effect. The limit is four trout; three fish under 13 inches and one over 22 inches, using artificial lures only. All grayling fishing on the Big Hole and its tributaries is catch-and-release.

To better understand the fishery on the Big Hole I will take you through the four seasons on the river, and share with you some experiences and information I have gathered over the years.

Spring

Winters in the Big Hole Valley can be quite severe. Temperatures are often brutal, dropping well below zero. When the upper river begins to thaw in spring, good fishing is not far off. In fact, you can fish much of the river whenever there is open water. Small nymphs such as Gold Ribbed Hare's Ears, Pheasant

Previous page: The Big Hole River as seen from the bridge which crosses it near Divide.

Tail or Prince nymphs in sizes 14 to 12 work well, as do caddis and stonefly nymphs in some of the faster water. Early in the season the fish don't seem to be too leader shy and you can get by using 3X tippet with most nymphs, which is nice in the event you hook a trophy-sized fish.

During early spring the water levels on the 'Hole will normally be low. Not like summertime lows, but low nonetheless. March will see a slight rise in the river, but it isn't until April and May that there is a significant increase in volume due to snow melt. Fishing during this time can be interesting. The upper river and its tributaries are good places to focus your attention, while there is ample water to fish them. It is also a time when you see few anglers on the river.

Spring hatches on the Big Hole start, as in most western rivers, with midges as soon as there is open water. If afternoons are particularly warm, trout will rise to the adults, even if there is still ice around the edges of the stream. Wire pupas such as the Brassie work well, as do many midge pupa imitations. For the adults on top, its hard to beat the Griffith's Gnat tied in size 16 or 18.

As the water rises and the temperatures warm in May, fishing picks up markedly. Caddis, small stoneflies and mayflies including the Blue-Winged Olive (BWO) make an appearance and offer fine angling to the dry fly fisherman. Although the river will continue to rise until it peaks in June, it doesn't usually get blown out of shape during the runoff period like many of the other Montana rivers. The 'Hole is naturally a bit off-colored due to its mineral content, but almost always remains fishable, except for short periods of extreme runoff associated with heavy mountain rains.

The meadow-like stretch of river between Wisdom and Wise River is enjoyable during this time of year and offers quite a diversity in its fishing. Here you can hook rainbows, brookies, cutthroat, whitefish, the occasional brown and grayling. In many places the river is channeled, and the wise angler will hit the deeper troughs and holding water in each channel before moving on. One blustery, late May afternoon last season I managed a Big Hole "grand slam," landing every species found in the river!

The section of river from the Salmon Fly Access at Melrose downstream to Brown's Bridge is a popular early season float. In this section you will find mostly browns, whitefish and a few rainbows. This is a fairly mellow section of stream and easy to float unless there is a particularly heavy runoff. There are all types of water found in this float; pools, riffles and long stretches of rock-bottomed stream—ideal habitat for feeding fish.

Hatches will be in full-swing by late April and May. The floating angler should pay special attention to the banks, foam lines and structure, making a point to anchor or get out and fish these areas thoroughly. Caddis and mayfly hatches can produce top-water feeding frenzies that trigger hot action to those who happen to be on the water when its going on. Nearly any caddis pattern properly presented this time of year in this stretch of river, is a safe bet.

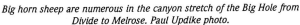

Big horn sheep are numerous in the canyon stretch of the Big Hole from Divide to Melrose. Paul Updike photo.

Irrigation of farmland along the Big Hole River near Divide.

During a normal year, with normal snow-melt and runoff, the salmonfly hatch will begin early to mid-June. Anglers descend upon the Big Hole in masses to take part in the frenzy. This is the busiest time of the year on the 'Hole, and the river can become quite crowded with boats as well as bank anglers. Outfitters from all over the state guide the Big Hole during the salmonfly hatch and, their presence, although legal, is quite the controversy among local guides.

Any large, adult salmonfly pattern will produce. Sofa Pillows, Stimulators, or basically any large, orange salmonfly pattern presented to a rising fish will result in an eager take, at least for the first part of the hatch. After a few days of intense angling pressure the fish wise up and it is the angler with the more exact imitation and presentation that catches the most fish. As the fish get more educated, tippet sizes need to be smaller to present the fly more naturally. This is where many anglers fail.

After the salmonfly hatch, fishing pressure on the 'Hole drops dramatically, even though angling is still very good. Just as before the salmonflies, caddis and mayfly hatches are abundant, and are pretty much widespread throughout the entire river. The mayflies you will encounter include March Browns, Gray Drakes, and PMD's.

Summer

June sees a major change in the flow of the river. Irrigation demand is heavy and, with the watershed drying up by late June like it has for the past several years, the flow of the 'Hole is greatly reduced, on average, from its peak of around 4,200 cfs at the first of the month, down to around 1,200 cfs by the end of June. Early summer fishing is good though. Caddis are the predominant hatch, with some smaller stoneflies and again, a variety of mayflies.

Mountains and antelope along Interstate 15 north of Melrose, after a fall storm.

◆

There are no special techniques needed for fishing the hatches on the 'Hole, but careful stalking and delicate presentations with light tippets will certainly pay off for the dry fly angler. By light tippets I don't mean 7X spring creek-light, you can almost always get by with 5X and, over extremely quiet water you may have to resort to 6X, but not often. More important, I believe, is the drag free float of your fly.

It is wise to remember that there are some real monsters in this river and the light tippets that produce "the most" strikes will most likely fail if you hook a true pig. its a bit of a trade-off; light tippet, dry fly—lots of fish or heavy tippet, big streamer— and maybe a trophy. It's a tough call sometimes, especially when you snap a large fish off that rose to your fly. What I like to do, especially when floating, is to have two rods rigged, one with a floating line and dry fly, the other with a big nymph or streamer. That way I can fish the water more thoroughly and up my odds of hooking Mr. Big.

Fisheries habitat of the Big Hole is adversely effected during periods of extreme low water flow. The extremely low flows of the river due to drought are compounded by dewatering for agricultural purposes. Low flows alone wouldn't be all that serious, but the warming that consequently occurs can be disastrous. For the past few years, besides not having a normal snowpack in the mountains, summer rains have been minimal. During a "normal" summer, the rain not only adds volume to the river, but

Previous page: Beautiful days and crisp autumn nights make an annual trip a must on the Big Hole Canyon section. Paul Updike photo.

helps cool the water which is very important for healthy survival of trout and grayling.

When the water is low, fishing is still quite good until the water temperatures get too high. By mid-summer, fishing along the banks with hopper patterns, as well as attractors like Humpies and Royal Trudes can produce some big-time excitement, especially in the sections of the river where brown trout are predominant. A big brown isn't too bashful when charging from an undercut bank to take a tasty morsel like a big 'ole hopper. But you must remember to cast very close to the streamside vegetation to get the fish's attention.

Another fly of importance in late summer is the *Tricorythodes* mayfly (*Trico*). At times fish will tune into this little mayfly and refuse all else. When this is the case, if you don't have any *Tricos* in your box you just might go fishless. And even if you do have some *Tricos*, you might go fishless because this is some of the most difficult fishing the river has to offer. Delicate, precise, drag-free presentations with fine tippets are a must.

Fall

Traditionally, fall is my favorite time on the water. And the Big Hole has been good to me in the fall. The period of time in fall when night temperatures have cooled the water down enough to make fish active again, all the way to ice-up can be a productive time for monster hunting.

In fall, *Baetis* mayflies can be important during hatches, which occur during the warmest part of the day. A tiny, number 18 or 20 BWO or Black *Baetis* can take a surprising number of fish if you find an area where a good hatch is coming off. Watch along the banks close to good holding water. Trout move to the edge of the faster current and sip in the small mayflies right on

◆

Tricorythodes (Trico) mayfly spent spinners. Hatches of small mayflies can be frustrating during the summer.

the current seam. Takes are often very subtle, so keep a close watch on your fly and leader.

You can find good *Baetis* beds along the entire river system. I prefer to fish the canyon stretch near Divide when the *Baetis* are on, and during the periods when nothing is hatching, I will bounce a nymph along the bottom through the deeper water with hopes it will find its way into the mouth of a big brown.

Although the *Baetis* hatches can be fun, most of the time during fall I like to use big streamers and Girdle Bugs, especially when fishing for big browns. One of my favorite ways to fish any river which holds browns is to cast weighted Girdle Bugs tight against the shore from a drifting boat. You can cover a lot of water doing this, and when rapidly stripped back from the bank, you can get the attention of feeding, as well as sulking fish. There is nothing delicate about this type of fishing. I usually go with a floating line and short leader of around six feet, tapered down to a fine, 1X tippet.

When not fishing from a boat I like to use a Teeny 130 grain sinking-tip line and cover the water using the basic down and across approach. Muddlers, Spuddlers, Matukas, Woolly Buggers—any large streamer can produce. If you work through a good looking section of river without results, change streamers and go through it again. Sometimes you need to change streamer color a few times until you find just the right one to trigger strikes.

As the water temperatures cool down below the 40 degree mark, trout will be harder to make contact with and whitefish hookups will be more frequent.

Whitlock Mouse. Mice patterns will take some of the larger trout near, or into, the darkness of night.

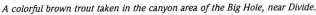

A colorful brown trout taken in the canyon area of the Big Hole, near Divide.

Winter

At times trout can be taken during winter months but are usually "incidental catches" by those fishing for whitefish. There are some monster whitefish in the Big Hole, and they seem to be very plentiful. There is an extended whitefish season on the Big Hole from December 1 to the third Saturday in May with maggots and/or artificial flies and lures only. Due to the abundance of these fish, the limit is 100. Keep in mind though, the section of river from Divide Dam to the Melrose Bridge is closed to all fishing during this period.

Although winters can be cold and river ice can interfere with fishing for whitefish, there are places on the stream where conditions let you fish for whitefish for a good part of the winter season. Catches by those targeting whitefish are usually high.

Tackle and Gear

*F*OR MOST FISHING ON THE BIG HOLE AN EIGHT TO nine foot, four or five-weight rod is a good choice. The exception would be when fishing large streamers down deep for the large browns which are found in the river. For this a six or seven-weight system would be the wiser choice, keeping in mind that some of the browns can exceed 10 pounds.

A weight-forward or double-taper floating line is probably the best all-around line, but if you plan on fishing large streamers in some of the deeper pools, a heavy sinking-tip line should be included in your arsenal. My favorite is a Teeny 130 grain sinking-tip, which allows me to dredge the deepest of pools.

Leaders are largely personal choice but just remember, after the salmonfly hatch fish can become gun shy, so to speak, and if your casts are met with an abnormal number of refusals, try lengthening your leader, using a smaller tippet size, or both.

For most of the season, neoprene waders are the most practical but during late summer/early fall, air and water temperatures can be high. Most anglers prefer to wade wet. Felt-soled wading shoes or cleats are a good idea regardless of the waders you use due to the slick, rock bottom found on the 'Hole.

Even though western Montana has been caught in the grips of an extended drought for several years now, expect extremes in weather when visiting here, and come prepared. During summer it can be dreadfully hot, but thunderstorms can rattle through with little warning, so rain gear is important baggage on your float even if you leave under clear blue skies. I know, I've been soaked more than once while on this river! Spring and fall can host cold weather whenever a front comes through. Keep in mind that the Big Hole flows from over 7,000 feet down to an elevation of 4,600 feet. Take a jacket along just in case!

◆

Winter comes early to the upper Big Hole Valley. Here ice forms on the river during late fall.

A frigid fall afternoon on the upper Big Hole.

Irresistible Temptation Orange   Steve's Salmon Fly
CDC Elk Caddis Dun   Hi-Vis Para-Caddis Olive   CDC Elk Caddis Brown   CDC Elk Caddis Black
Elk Hair Caddis Brown   CDC Caddis   No Hackle BWO   No Hackle PMD   Trico
Green Hackle Extended Compara-Dun   Gray Drake Extended Compara-Dun   PMD Extended Compara-Dun
Parachute Adams   SRI Crystal Wing Wulff   Red Humpy   Yellow Humpy
Royal Coachman Trude   Dave's Hopper   Hi-Vis Foam Ant

S.R. Woolhead Sculpin Olive   S.R. Woolhead Black
Woolly Bugger Olive   Woolly Bugger Brown   Woolly Bugger Black
Girdle Bug   SRI Superior Stone Fly   SRI Superior Stone Fly Black-Giant
SRI Superior Stone Fly Brown-Giant   Bow River Bugger
Black Marabou Muddler   White Marabou Muddler   Muddler Minnow
Zug Bug   Pheasant Tail   Gold Ribbed Hare's Ear   Bead Head Prince   Brassie

Salmonfly imitations. The Big Hole has a tremendous hatch of these big stoneflies that bring anglers from all over the country.

◆

Suggested Fly Patterns

*I*T WOULD BE VERY HARD—NO, IMPOSSIBLE—TO LIST every fly pattern that would be effective when fishing the Big Hole River. There are only X-number of aquatic and terrestrial insects important in trout fishing, and a million patterns to imitate them, with a million more variations.

We all show up on the stream with boxes stuffed to the brim with flies and most of them would probably work at one time or another. What I will do is provide you with a list of my favorites; patterns that I consistently use on the 'Hole and the logic (if there is any) behind why I use them. All of the flies listed here are featured in the fly plate.

Dries

Hi-Vis Para-Caddis (olive): This is a great pattern during low light, water conditions where it is hard to see your fly, or when the fish are selective, this is a good fly if olive caddisflies are present. Sizes: No. 12 to No. 16.

CDC Elk Caddis (dun, brown, black): This is a high-floating caddis imitation that works well in all types of water, whenever the appropriate color of caddisfly is present. Sizes: No. 12 to No. 16.

Elk Hair Caddis (brown): A more standard, yet productive caddis pattern. Can be tied in any color to match the caddisflies present. Sizes: No. 10 to No. 18.

CDC Caddis: Hard to beat when tiny, dark caddisflies are on the water. Sizes: No. 18 to No. 20.

Humpy (red, yellow): The Humpy is a good attractor that doesn't specifically imitate anything, but certainly catches its share of fish in the Big Hole as well as other western rivers. Sizes: No. 10 to No. 14.

Irresistible Temptation (orange): This is a good fly when the salmonfly hatch is on. It floats well and is durable, standing up to many fish. Sizes: No. 6 to No. 10.

Steve's Salmon Fly: This is my own salmonfly pattern. It doesn't float as well as the Irresistible Temptation, but it is realistic looking and if fish are hot on the hatch they gobble this fly up before it sinks. Grease it well! Sizes: No. 6 to No. 10.

Parachute Adams: Not much to say about this fly that hasn't already been said a million times. It's simply one of the best all-around dry flies ever created. Sizes: No. 10 to No. 22.

Green Drake Extended Compara-Dun: A very realistic Green Drake mayfly pattern. Size: No. 12.

Gray Drake Extended Compara-Dun: A good choice when gray or dull-colored mayflies are on the water. Sizes: No. 14 to No. 20.

BWO Extended Compara-Dun: Great when BWOs are present. Sizes: No. 16 to No. 20.

PMD Extended Compara-Dun: My favorite when the appropriate sized PMDs are on the water. Sizes: No. 14 to No. 20.

No Hackle BWO: This is a good BWO pattern for stillwater when the fish are demanding. Sizes: No. 16 to No. 22.

No Hackle PMD: Same as with the BWO, a great fly when the fish are picky. Sizes: No. 16 to No. 22.

Royal Coachman Trude: This is a good attractor during those times when nothing is hatching, especially when floated along a shoreline during the summer. Sizes: No. 10 to No. 14.

Dave's Hopper: Hard to beat during summer when hoppers are present. Cast tight against the banks. Sizes: No. 8 to No. 12.

Tricorythodes: Fishing *Tricos* can make the difference between success and failure. If you don't have a few of these in your box when they are the only thing hatching, you will most likely be out of luck. Sizes: No. 16 to No. 22.

SRI Crystal Wing Wulff: This fly is great when fishing small mayfly hatches in low light situations. Sizes: No. 12 to No. 16.

Hi-Vis Foam Ant: This is an outrageous ant pattern. It floats well, you can see it and trout love it. What else can I say? Sizes: No. 12 to No. 20

Nymphs

Bead Head Prince: A standard favorite on many western rivers. Sizes: No. 12 to No. 16.

Gold Ribbed Hare's Ear: Probably the best nymph ever created. When tied in different sizes this fly resembles many aquatic insects. Sizes: No. 10 to No. 20.

Pheasant Tail: Another standard that resembles several insects. Sizes: No. 10 to No. 20.

Brassie: One of the best pupae imitations for taking fussy trout. Sizes: No. 18 to No. 22.

Zug Bug: This is another of the standard nymphs that resembles several mayfly nymphs and other aquatic food items. Sizes: No. 10 to No. 20.

SRI Superior Stonefly (regular size and giant; black or brown): These are realistic, durable and fast-sinking stonefly patterns perfect for dredging the bottom looking for Mr. Big.

Streamers

Black Marabou Muddler: When dredging for big browns, this fly is a killer. Sizes: No. 10 to No. 2.

White Marabou Muddler: Just as with the Black Muddler, fish this fly deep. Sizes: No. 2 to No. 10.

Muddler Minnow: This is a standard sculpin pattern that is still one of the best around. Sizes: No. 2 to No. 10.

Bead Head Woolly Bugger (olive, brown, black): If you only take one streamer to the Big Hole, or to any river for that matter, make sure it is the Woolly Bugger. There is none better! Sizes: No. 2 to No. 10.

S.R. Woolhead Sculpin (brown, black): Dredging the bottom with this critter will get the attention of big trout as well as

As with many places, some of the largest brown trout are taken after dark. Steve Probasco prepares to release a big brown that fell to a mouse pattern.

Charlie Busteed fishing the middle Big Hole during the spring.

◆

your angling partners if it gets too close to them. Size: No. 4.

Girdle Bug When floating the river during fall I like to cast this fly into the bank and strip back quickly. This drives trout— especially browns—nuts! Sizes: No. 4 to No. 10.

Fisheries Management

*T*HE MONTANA DEPARTMENT OF FISH, WILDLIFE AND Parks has an ongoing plan to preserve and enhance the Big Hole River's fishery. In the September 1989-September 1994 Fisheries Management Plan, prepared by the Department, many issues regarding the fishery are considered. I will share a few of the highlights, and a few observations of my own.

First off, the study revealed that as a result of the extreme low water during the summer and fall of 1988, electrofishing during the spring of 1989 showed that 50-60 percent of the one and two year old fish were eliminated from the population. The study also revealed that a significant number of surviving fish were severely stressed.

The Department had hoped to develop a plan to increase flows during the low water periods. The problem is that, at present, during times of extremely low water flow, the problem is worsened by water diversions for irrigation. There are not many

options open to the Department. Outdated water rights by irrigators overrule the desperate need to keep as much water in the river as possible.

The Department is working hard, however, in an attempt to find a solution for the problem. A few things the Department is doing are: Working closely with individual land owners and Conservation Districts by encouraging conservation, working with the Water Quality Bureau (DHES) to insure that water quality standards are enforced, working closely with the Forest Service and the BLM regarding mining, timber and grazing, exploring the possibility of offstream or tributary storage and water leasing, and several other items along the same line. The Department had hoped that by the end of 1994 there would be at least a partial solution to the problem of low water flows.

About the possibility of offstream or tributary storage, this was investigated by the Montana Department of Natural Resources (DNRC) at the request of the State Legislature. The study started in 1977 and the final report came in January of 1981. The study recommended that a dam be built on Pattengail Creek which is 12 miles south of Wise River. It is the opinion of most people I have talked with that this project will probably never fly for political reasons.

The DNRC also suggested renting water rights from irrigators so that instream flows could be increased. However, when the Bill was introduced in 1989 it was not passed by the Legislature. As of this writing, during the last month of 1994, the

Department is still working on the problem of water flow during the summer and fall months on the Big Hole.

During the severe water shortages of 1994, the Department worked closely with land owners along the upper Big Hole and according to Dick Oswald, they were met with cooperation from irrigators in keeping more water flowing in the main channel. "The problem is far from being solved, and the whole key, until the end of the drought," says Dick Oswald, "is cooperation."

Prior to 1974, the Big Hole was annually planted with catchable-size hatchery rainbows. Research during the 70s indicated that hatchery plants were actually detrimental to the wild stocks of rainbow. In 1974 almost all planting was eliminated. Brown trout numbers today average more than double what they were during the planting days, and rainbow trout numbers have almost tripled.

In 1981 the section of river between Divide and Melrose was placed under special regulations. The "slot limit" which was adopted stated that trout between 13 and 22 inches be released. The results of this new regulation suggested that the numbers of large brown trout increased, as did the size of all rainbows. However, those rainbows over 16 inches didn't increase in proportion to the browns, probably due to the higher number of rainbows.

Grayling fishing on the Big Hole became catch-and-release in 1988. The grayling have a tough road ahead, but after plummeting to an estimated 22 fish per mile in 1987, the grayling seem to be holding their own. Many factors will decide the fate of these last river-dwelling grayling in the lower 48. The Department lists them as a "Species of Special Concern", and most fishery management decisions on the Big Hole revolve around saving the species.

The Department anticipates that public use of the Big Hole will increase in the future. Conflicts between users, agriculture and recreation, including increased commercial (outfitter) use, are all topics of great concern and are being addressed at the present time.

Mule deer dot the Big Hole slopes year-round. Paul Updike photo.

Ken Bamford with an "average" rainbow from nearby Clark Canyon Reservoir, which is the start of the Beaverhead River.

The Surrounding Area

*T*HERE IS SO MUCH TO DO IN SOUTHWESTERN Montana and in the general vicinity of the Big Hole River, when planning a trip to this area you should plan on taking a few extra days to spend fishing a few other famous waters within a few hours' drive from the Big Hole.

You could easily spend all of your time fishing the 'Hole, there are miles of prime trout water. In addition, many of the tributaries are great fishing in their own right and are worthy of some special attention, but they get little because of the quality water close by.

The Big Hole joins the Beaverhead near Twins Bridges, some 155 miles from the Big Hole's source. If you were to follow the Beaverhead upstream 79 miles you would come to its source. The Beaverhead, especially the upper 16 miles of river, is also classified as a blue ribbon stream. Although it is a much smaller river, the Beaverhead has been said to host more large fish per mile than any other river in Montana.

Following page: You can find solitude in the fall on the Big Hole.
Paul Updike photo.

A barbed-wire fence crosses the Big Hole near Wisdom. Fences are a hazard to floaters on the upper river.

◆

The Beaverhead begins as the outflow of Clark Canyon Reservoir, another quality water within an hour or so from the Big Hole. Fly fishing for chunky rainbows and browns draws anglers from far and wide. Float tubing the reservoir produces trout that average a few pounds and grow into the teens.

The city of Dillon is the largest "big" town in this part of Montana. Dillon is a good starting point for fishing several waters in this area. There are a couple of fly shops in Dillon, Fishing Headquarters, (406)683-6660, and Fountier Anglers, (406)683-5276. Either one of these shops will be happy to let you know what's hot in the area at the moment.

From Dillon, it is only a couple of hours to the Madison River, an hour to the Ruby or the Jefferson, three hours from West Yellowstone, the Henry's Fork, and . . . well, you get the picture.

But back to the Big Hole. With the exception of the recent, extreme water shortages during the late summer, you can easily fish a different section of the Big Hole every day of your visit. When planning a trip, a fly shop that I recommend, located in the town of Melrose, is Montana Trophy Anglers, (406)835-3071. Phil Smith, who recently passed on, along with his daughter Georgia, ran the shop, guided and basically knew as much about the river as anyone. Phil had over three decades worth of knowledge on the Big Hole. He has seen the river through good and

bad. Phil is a large part of what the Big Hole and its fishing is today and our hats are off to him. By calling or stopping by the shop you can get the skinny on what's going on where.

In addition to Montana Trophy Anglers in Melrose, there are several fly shops, outfitters and guide services located along the Big Hole that can help with any of your questions on a guide, flies, etc. Also, the fly shops in Butte (only about an hour away) can answer all of your questions, line you up with a guide, etc. Finding out what's happening in this part of Montana is not a hard thing to do.

The Big Hole is many things to many people. To me, it is one of Montana's finest trout streams and that is why I keep going back. But besides fishing, the area offers kayaking, hunting, rockhounding, gold panning, as well as rock climbing in the Humbug Spires.

Wildlife along the Big Hole is abundant, with large populations of deer, elk and antelope. Black bears are common in the upper valley, but there is no grizzly habitat. One of the largest winter ranges for moose in Montana is between Wisdom and Ralston.

Of course, there are smaller animals along the river, beaver, mink, and otter being the most ineresting, as well as a myriad of birds, including a variety of waterfowl. Rattlesnakes are common from Divide downstream, so beware!

The Future

*T*HE BIG HOLE'S REPUTATION AS A WORLD CLASS RIVER, Class I, blue ribbon stream, or whatever name for choice, productive trout water you want to call it, is well deserved. Over the years, this river's ability to withstand seemingly, unsurmountable odds has proven its durability. Its grayling are the last of a breed—as the saying goes. But will the grayling and the Big Hole's trout fishery survive? This is a question that is well deserved in the asking.

Angler use of the Big Hole is very high. In a study entitled "The Net Economic Value of Fishing in Montana" the Big Hole was found to be one of the highest valued streams in Montana. And in a companion study entitled "Angler Preference Survey" the Montana Department of Fish, Wildlife and Parks learned much about the Big Hole's anglers. The study year was the summer of 1986.

A total of 185 residents and non-residents were mailed questionnaires and 85 percent were returned. Approximately 70 percent of those surveyed were residents and 30 percent were non-residents. The majority, about 71 percent fished from shore, and 29 percent used a boat. Five percent used a guide or outfitter. Eleven percent indicated they were bait fishermen. Seventeen percent indicated they saw more fishermen than they expected to see. However, 83 percent said that their fishing was unaffected by other anglers. Of those that said they were affected, 29 percent said it was competition for holes that bothered them most, while 18 percent said the problem was floating related. "Too many boats" and "water levels" were also major complaints. Over 65 percent said that the Big Hole was either their favorite, or one of their favorite, streams in Montana. Regarding questions on management, most people preferred habitat protection and special regulations with limited kill; size and gear restrictions topped concerns.

Tourism and recreation is Montana's number two industry. Fishing of the blue ribbon trout streams is a major part of this industry. Statistics compiled by the Department of Fish, Wildlife and Parks in 1986 showed that non-resident use of the Big Hole was 30 percent of all fishermen in that year. In 1987, the Department released a study authored by John Duffield of the University of Montana, John Loomis of the University of California, Davis, and Rob Brooks of the Department. The study showed that trips on the Big Hole were among the highest val-

Fall colors invade the high country as early as September.

Rainbow trout taken from the middle Big Hole. The largest trout are found further downstream.

◆

Although common sense says, hey . . . watch out, there is trouble in the air, we choose, as a politically-controlled whole, to ignore the warning signs. Doesn't history teach us well? Why are the warning signs on the Big Hole, printed in black and white, ignored?

Some will argue that the Big Hole and its fishing has survived OK. Agricultural dewatering has been going on since "civilized" man settled the Big Hole Valley and the river keeps bouncing back from man's misuse. That attitude, to coin a phrase by my teenage son, is lame! It's like racial segregation prior to the 1960s, it goes on because it always has, but it's not right. If the drought of recent years continues, combined with the rape by agricultural dewatering, the Big Hole will fall. The native grayling will be gone forever—the loss of which our nation should mourn. Every day on this planet, animal species needlessly and carelessly disappear forever, largely in the name of cold, hard cash. Money is to be made; the all-mighty dollar rules!

I once asked a Federal employee, hired to protect and preserve the struggling grayling fishery on the Big Hole, why there were no conservation-minded, regulatory rules for the ranchers on the Big Hole to follow, and why a certain few continue to use the Big Hole's water with reckless abandon without considering the "big picture." His reply was simply—"because they can."

We have seen many antiquated land user/owner rights permanently alter ecosystems in this country, as well as around the planet. When will enough be enough? When will we stand up as a whole and say, OK, here is the right thing to do. Many of our nation's natural treasures have been lost . . . forever! I only hope, as do many others, that Montana's magnificent, Big Hole River, and its struggling grayling don't join the list. Please, write your Congressmen. Pray for rain, do a little rain dance. The Big Hole needs and deserves it.

◆

Nymph assortment.

ued trips in the state and were valued at $164 per trip. Total recreational value for the Big Hole was estimated to be $5.2 million per year, and keep in mind that this was in 1987. The increase in interest in fly fishing since that time has made a significant jump, as fly fishing is one of the fastest growing sports in the nation. With such statistics, one has to wonder why the sport fishery doesn't have more of an impact on the status and future of politics regarding the Big Hole's fishery.

It would seem obvious to those of sound mind that the good of the river would reflect the feelings of the majority. If not morally, economically. The $5.2 million spent annually on recreation revolving around the Big Hole River should speak for itself. Why then, do outdated water rights, and grandfathering-in practices of water users on this river (as well as many Montana rivers) weigh so high? Politics, that's why!

Being from the Pacific Northwest, I base my views on local issues. Salmon and steelhead have suffered greatly from the greed of man. Careless, economically-motivated logging, commercial and native fishing rights have taken a toll on the fishery.

An angler fishing a section of the middle Big Hole during the spring.

Big Hole River Specifics

River Source: Skinner Lake, Beaverhead Mountains

Source Elevation: 7,340 feet

River Length: 155 miles

River Ends: Joins the Beaverhead River near Twin Bridges, Montana to form the Jefferson River

Elevation at Confluence with Beaverhead River: 4,600 feet

Big Hole Drainage Basin: 2,476 square miles

Watershed: Beaverhead, Pioneer and Anaconda Mountains, Dickie Hills, Highland Mountains

Drainage: Jefferson River to Missouri River to Mississippi River, to the Gulf

Annual Average Discharge: (measured near Melrose) 1,174 cubic feet per second

Maximum and Minimum Recorded Flows:
High: 23,000 cfs., 1927   Low: 49 cfs. August, 1931

First Permanent Settlers: 1880s

Major Land Uses (Big Hole Basin): Agriculture, timber and recreation

End of Hatchery Planting: 1974

Catch-and-Release Status for Grayling: 1988

Major Fish Species: Rainbow trout, brook trout, brown trout, cutthroat trout, mountain whitefish, Montana grayling

Fishing Regulations: Standard daily and possession limit; five trout; only one over 18 inches
Exceptions: Entire river and its tributaries—catch-and-release for grayling, brook trout limit is 20 fish, whitefish limit is 100.
Tributaries upstream from Divide Dam open entire year for brook trout.
Special Slot Limit Areas: Dickie Bridge to Divide Dam, four trout limit; three fish under 13 inches and one over 22 inches with artificial flies and lures only.

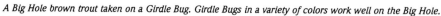

A Big Hole brown trout taken on a Girdle Bug. Girdle Bugs in a variety of colors work well on the Big Hole.

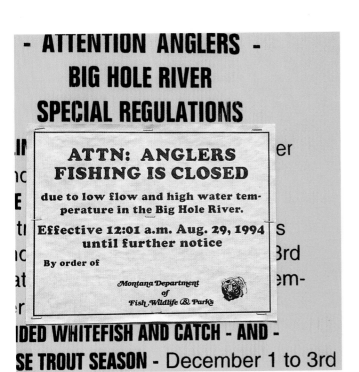

- ATTENTION ANGLERS -
BIG HOLE RIVER
SPECIAL REGULATIONS

**ATTN: ANGLERS
FISHING IS CLOSED**

due to low flow and high water temperature in the Big Hole River.

**Effective 12:01 a.m. Aug. 29, 1994
until further notice**

By order of

Montana Department
of
Fish, Wildlife & Parks

IDED WHITEFISH AND CATCH - AND -
SE TROUT SEASON - December 1 to 3rd

*Closure notice posted during the summer of 1994 when the river was
closed due to low flows and high water temperatures.*

Special whitefish season and catch-and-release for trout:
open Dec. 1 to the third Saturday in May with maggots
and/or flies and lures.
Divide Dam to Melrose Bridge: Also under the
"slot limit" regulations but all fishing is closed from Dec. 1
to the third Saturday in May

Floatable: 139 miles (under ideal water conditions)

Floating Skills Needed: Intermediate to
experienced

Dangers: Diversion dams, fences (upper river),
irrigation jetties

Special Boating Regulations: No motors on entire river

Access: Good. Road parallels river with numerous
access sites

Services: Limited in Jackson, Wisdom, Wise River,
Melrose, Glen and Twin Bridges. All services in Dillon

Camping: Brown's Bridge, Salmon Fly, Maiden Rock,
Divide, Dickie Bridge, Bryant Creek Road, Sportsman
Park, Fishtrap Creek

Fly Shops/Outfitters: Several shops/outfitters
along the river. Fly shops/outfitters guiding the river
located in Melrose, Dillon, Butte and other southwestern
Montana towns/cities

Boat Ramps: High Road, Notch Bottom, Glen Bridges,
Brown's Bridge, Salmon Fly, Maiden Rock, Divide, Divide
Dam, Dewey, Jerry Creek, Dickie Bridge, Sportsman Park,
Fishtrap Creek, Squaw Creek, Doolittle Creek. Also available are many access points where public lands adjoin the
river

Flow Information: USGS (406)449-5263

Maps Available:
BLM: #31 Big Hole (upper) #32 Dillon (lower)
USFS: Beaverhead National Forest
USGS: Dillon
"Montana Afloat"
"Montana Atlas & Gazetteer" (DeLorme Mapping Company)

Ken Bamford fishing the middle section of the Big Hole.

The Big Hole River as seen from the bridge near Divide.